Spirits in the Forest

A collection of poetry

Kevin McManus

Spirits in the Forest

Kevin McManus

Published by Wolfmoon Press, 2024.

SPIRITS IN THE FOREST

First edition. April 1, 2024.

ISBN: 979-8224134571

Written by Kevin McManus.

As far as we can discern, the sole purpose of human existence is to kindle a light in the darkness of mere being.

Carl Jung

KEVIN MCMANUS

Everything was this moment

The white sash window was open slightly,
it was early May.
The net curtain waltzed back and forth
like the swash and backwash of a wave,
as the early, fresh and clean Summer air
flowed in.
It was quiet, almost silent apart from
birdsong from the tree in the garden and
the flutter of the green leaves.
The afternoon light that shone through
the curtain landed on a spot on the brown
flower-patterned carpet.
Everything was in harmony,
everything was this moment.

Lost change from strangers

It's closing time,
all the dead men gathered on the counter,
sweeping the evening from the floor,
fag butts and memories,
lost change from strangers,
for the poor box,
dogs for the blind
drunk at the bar
arguing
with himself.
Mary Black is past the point of rescue
on the jukebox in the corner,
a sleeping soul on a low seat,
longing for a soft bed and sanctuary
and a soft touch no longer there.
Spider webs sway
on forgotten crepe paper illuminations,
smoke and stale beer hang in the air,
hailstones against the window,
devils at the door.

A Pagan Place

On hallowed ground,
Where the whitethorn meets the blackthorn,
a threshold through the spiritual veil.
When you are with nature you are with the earth,
walking through a living landscape
feeling the spirit of the country,
We change in the thin places
we connect in those liminal spaces.
The veil is thin at the borderlands.
at the forest edge,
light coming through the trees,
casting upon the sacred oak,
beside flowing river water,
over rocks and boulders,
by the sea as the waves meet the shore.
A connection with those
who were rooted to the same places in the past,
to the people of the mounds,
the hill of Uisneach,
Tara, Bru na Boinne,
Knocknarea, Carrowmore
Rathcroghan, the cave of cats,
into the womb of the world.
The soul of the Caileach embodied
in the hallowed places.
Magic is hiding in plain sight.
Spirits move from the outer and inner worlds.
The curtain is translucent
over the three days and nights of Samhain.
To be open and receptive,

to pull deep within the grove of trees,
transcendence in the temenos.

Lost souls

Sitting alone at the bar in Kilburn,
mid-afternoon on a mid-Summers day
wearing a suit stained with blood,
sweat and booze,
drinking the last of this month's rent.
He took the boat in 57'
leaving behind Mayo,
full of hope and fear,
an address in his pocket,
for a ganger and a start,
money for a week to tide him over,
Sunday best on his back,
new shoes squeezing his feet.
No Irish need apply,
lodgings hard found,
working every hour God sent,
paid in the crown at the weekend,
missing home, laughs to hide the pain,
another from the top shelf.
Saving for the summer holiday,
putting a little by,
back home for a week to the old sod,
buying pints for the lads,
bragging about the wages,
gold chains around the neck,
bought from a suitcase.
When did you get home?
When are you going back?
Back to back breaking in blighty,
years passing on,

body getting tired,
drink taking hold,
no money for the holidays,
or the funerals at home.
Nights in the doss house,
sleeping on the rope,
days on the streets,
dreams of a long-gone family,
passing away in the cold.

Where does the light go when the candle is blown out?

Life begins in the dark and grows into the light,
a word is the son of two fathers
carved out of the shadows,
when the night become morning.
Searching for a sense of self
in the quiet places,
where the river flows within
the spaces shaped by the silence.
The wind and rain carry
the whispers of the land
and songs of solitude and awakening,
the only barrier is our willingness.

The clearance

Ghosts in the long grass,
cold hunger winds bearing down
on the voiceless people,
from homes long since crumbled,
the great clearance of the unwanted.

There is magic and beauty around us

There is magic and beauty that surrounds us,
if we stop to listen,
if we stop to stare,
but our perception have been blunted,
our emotions have been stunted,
drowned out by modernity,
and our focus on internity,
there is magic and beauty that surrounds us,
it floats around us and abides in us.

Opened ground

The smell of opened earth,
stained with blood and diesel dripping down.
The drone of the engine,
the clatter of the arm as it dug,
breaking through old stone shores
laid by large, strong hands.
Red sparks and white ash
floating upwards towards the sky,
carried by black smoke,
from burning whin bush and branch
Held down as the flames consumed them.
A body in a cold wet drain,
bent low with pick, bar, spade and shovel.
Straightening up, taking a breather,
a swallow of cold tea from a bottle,
a bite of dry soda bread
from a piece of wrapped cloth.
Stretching a tall, tired frame,
clearing the sweat and dried daub from a lined furrow.
Old for his age, landless,
labouring in another man's field.
Taken too soon,
a man I never met.

The sky was crying

Looking up through a twisted hazel
the sky was crying
tears.
The streaming of the ancient rain,
down fractured walls and windowpane,
and played on the roof like a drum
the wind sang a song from the rain.
An outpouring falling slowly
on the earth to invigorate and nurture
the grey sea and long black land.
The healing therapy of tears
a universal grieving for all those lost.
And after the rain,
after the deluge,
the scent of the soil.
A gentle drip from an emerald leaf
the parting of the heavens
and restoration of the sun
as the healing arises.

Before the Storm

Barriers, barricades boarded up
waiting for the storm to rise.
The uplift, the surge,
ropes are tightened, they hold fast,
they creak and moan as the strain comes upon them.
Forecast on the radio,
hands are held in prayer,
rosary beads entwined around bony fingers,
heads bowed,
a gentle murmuring,
the sign of the cross,
relics are kissed.
The wind elevates,
the pressure grows
a perfect storm,
dark clouds overhead,
carry torrents of tension,
the fear of the unknown,
uncertainty and apprehension.
The clock ticks forward,
the storm passes,
a cleansing prevails,
lessons are learned,
clarity shines brighter.

On Garadice shore

Going over old ground past the church,
under the low Winter sun towards the
shoreline,
the green mossed stone and the bare black
branches.
At years end, time passed.
lucid thoughts that pierce through
the empty spaces,
these things will stay with you.
A bell rings across the lake,
calling patrons to prayer,
to try and make sense of self,
to be rooted to this old ground
on a lake shore.

When the evening shadows fall

One by one the lights came on
within the misty hollow glen.
Headlights climbed the hilly roads
that knew the place to go.
Coats and scarves hung on a hook
as the evening work was done.
Kettles boiled and table set,
schoolbooks pushed aside.
No head was raised as the angelus chimed
a grace was shared within.
Evening news sat side by side
around a hearth aglow.

On the dark days of December

On a dark morning in December,
the sky was wet and heavy with clouds,
the branches hung low and draped
towards the grey water,
a black tweed cap was perched on the ash,
the grass laid lank and flat,
it was bleached by frost,
the moon was still up, its crescent
partially hidden behind a cloud
even though it was gone eight,
thoughts were centred on the days to come
and not the here and now,
the faces were turned towards the earth
as we waited,
as we waited on the dark days of December.

Solstice, the feast of the risen Sun

The shortest day, the darkness
before the dawn,
celebrating light in the blackness
of mid-Winter,
for the ancients a time of cold and hunger,
the rebirth of Mitra, the old sun is dead,
the new one is rising.
Its power will grow stronger now
with each passing day.
Our forefathers marked this day
well with their earth mounds
which captured the blessed light
and warmed the frozen earth.
Bringing the evergreen inside, a symbol
that Spring will return.
The fire of the Yule log to sanctify
the dying year.
Odin's nocturnal flights,
the slaughter of the animals for
the Winter feast,
to keep up the strength for the harshest
months to come,
before the green shoots of life,
break through the cold ground once more,
the cycle continues, the wheel keeps turning.

Candle

On the eve of Christmas,
in the window a single wax candle,
frost carves gentle patterns upon the pane,
a yellow flame that dances in December air,
a light to guide lost souls that journey
the cold and silent roads outside.

On all the bare places

Imprints left behind where children
had frolicked,
carved out snow angels,
hollows filling with fresh powder,
that whispered and capered as it descended
upon the silent, frozen earth,
flakes falling everywhere,
on the glittering pines,
on ice sheltering a lake,
on silent drifts,
on all the bare places,
snow crystals maintained
their subtle dance,
wafting sideways
on the gentle stream of a breeze,
until a white mantle would
conceal and hide everything and nothing,
as if a landscape had vanished
into a silent snowbound domain,
where the Winter powered over all.

From fractures in the heavens

October, the colours, sounds, scents,
the bite of the coming cold,
a time of balance,
Samhain the veil between the spirit
and mortal world,
thin and transparent.
Loose glass panes rattled,
a stiff gust dashed
heavy drops of water upon them
like a heavenly blessing.
morning had delivered a chill
it swept away the heavy air.
Mountains folded upon the vale
like groups of giant monarchs
protecting that sacred ground.
A hint of blue was peering
through the weakening stratus cloud
from fractures in the heavens above.
Shards of light
cut through the grey and solemn shade
to heat the autumn earth
Ivy strangled the birch.
green foliage sparkled and glistened
as it danced in the light.
Sycamores released golden brown leaves,
they floated almost completely silent,
only making a gentle sound
as they gracefully touched the naked branches
before falling to earth to decompose
to provide new life

for the cycle that would begin again.

Thaddeus and Eleanor danced after the storm

Thaddeus stood at his doorway observing
the formation of an all engulfing storm.
He was no longer satisfied with silence
or listening to the gentle sound of rain
tinkling against his window,
lulling him to sleep.
He wanted new challenges,
new tumults to ascend.
Thaddeus awaited the scream of the wind,
above him his eyes lifted
to the stratus skyline,
the wind surged forward and
endlessly pounded like hammer blows
upon the earth,
overhead in darkening skies,
cadaverous clouds streamed
in abundant chaos.
Thaddeus welcomed the storm;
in fact, he embraced it and danced
within its swirling torrents.
In a previous life he battled it,
he outstretched his arms and cursed it,
the storm appeared never-ending to him,
it was all consuming,
waiting to devour him,
he was pulled into the deluge and sank
into the black depths of the dark water
as he struggled to swim,

to stay alive as the unremitting waves
battered him,
to fight against it appeared futile,
but he learned to endure the lash,
the agony of its rampant fury.
Thaddeus learned how to stop fighting it;
the more he resisted the further he sank,
Thaddeus learned how to float.
His saviour was Eleanor,
she taught him how to ride the storm,
to ride the crashing waves of the tempest,
she gave him safe harbour
in the volatile chaos that was his life before,
a shelter from the swelling seas,
a comforting light of hope
that guided him home past jagged reefs
into the arms of a nurturing cove,
her voice was soothing to him,
her words like the melody
of a familiar song
he had heard before
but couldn't quite remember where.
When the storm was over
and the carnage complete,
when the corpses had been counted
and the branch was on the bough,
Eleanor took Thaddeus by the hand
as they transcended light and shade,
they ethereally floated,
spectres on the shrill breeze
beyond time and latitude,
With no earthly constraints to hold them

to root them to the ground,
they rose together elegantly upwards to glide upon the heavenly currents.
When Eleanor took Thaddeus by the hand,
they danced after the storm.

The gloaming

Inside,
shadows silently slide
across the grey floor,
climb up the papered wall
and darken the window.
Outside,
the dusk hangs on the withered tree,
its limbs slashed, mutilated and torn.
Barbed wire twisted around its torso.
Piercing deep wounds into its old decaying bark.
Above,
a murder of crows swarm,
a dark dance against the dying evening light,
a chorus of their shrill harsh caw,
before reposing on high oak branches.
Beyond,
over the brown heathered hill,
the setting sun casts its colours,
an orange glow across the heavens,
then steals away to ascend again.

Spring moon

New moon blessings sailing above,
shines bright like a beacon
of new beginnings, new hope.

Ostara, the gathering of the light

The vernal equinox,
a period of equality and balance,
deadlock and stalemate,
night and day,
light and dark,
inside and outside,
man and woman.
A hallowed conjugal
the young Sun God has growing power,
the Earth Goddess has warmed and is awake,
fertility has been reborn,
rebirth and renewal,
the gorse and the violet.
the woodruff and the narcissus
the colours and the bird song
the hare and the egg.

A cobalt Sunday

A walk on a beautiful cobalt Sunday,
two butterflies danced
and followed me all the way.
A sky flawless and pure,
fragile threads of cloud marbled throughout.
Beckoned by the birdsong
and the silence spaces between.
The old mill house, a stone shrine
to the labours of the past.
A path that coils and arches
upon itself,
lined by the yellow clarion of Spring,
the daffodil.
Splendid isolation near a holy well,
blessed waters reservoir,
a place of peace and hope
a solace that is serene and still.

A dying fire

Morning light from an opened window
streaming down
a face hiding from yesterday,
and fearful of the forthcoming.
A memory ingrained too deep to purge,
that has impaired the spirit.
Waiting for a hunger
to fill the barren times once more.
A transitory touch of warmth,
the ephemeral nature of being,
like the evanescent glimmering of a cinder
in a dying fire on a cold morning in a kitchen
the traces and recollections of a night before.

Easter

A time of change and transition,
the sun climbs higher,
the light grows stronger,
life springs from dead winter branches,
regrowth, rebirth and renewal.
The swallow on the wing,
the call of the cuckoo,
a herald for fine weather.
The shower of petals,
like snow in April,
streaming from the Haw thorn,
ablaze with white blossoms.
In hedgerows creation abounds,
a wildfire of colours.
In the meadow the lamb,
life like blood rising,
a sacred icon of sacrifice and awakening.

May 17th, half light

Leaving the dark behind,
stumbling into the half light
of early dawn.
Waiting,
catching breath,
on a bench near Portobello Bridge,
silver skin on canal waters,
a golden hue everywhere,
a life ahead of me.
A moment
ingrained in the memory,
but only a fleeting glance,
transitory and impermanent,
in a dreamy half light.

Rain tree crow

Clouds heavy with rain
hovering low on the skyline,
the force growing as the storm encroaches.
On an open plain a solitary oak,
holding the ground resilient like a lone sentinel,
awaiting the thunderous hoofs
of the horseman charge,
the sacred oak stands firm as the heavens unleashes its tempest upon it,
that will bend the ancient bough, but it will not break.

Where angels whisper

Listening to the wind heaving at night,
the rain tapping against the window,
in daylight, feeling the breeze across your face,
the cold touch on your arm on a frosty morning,
the warm sun on your skin on a June afternoon,
the spray from the sea as you stand and stare,
the calmness you feel beside a lake,
the bird song at dawn,
the noise of the brown leaves under your feet in October,
These are the places where angels whisper.

The hawthorn tree

Sceach Gheal,
Unyielding and vigorous tree
that outlives mortal man.
Guardian of holy wells and thresholds,
but is never brought indoors.
Flowers in May in white and red,
a herbal cure to heal a broken heart.
The Witches' tree,
haws ripen at Samhain,
secrete a pungent odour of decay.
The sidhe dwells within the fairy bush
at night they sing their beguiling songs.
A portal gate to the otherworld,
crafted by its warped bough.
A lone tree that cannot be cut down
without suffering a faerie curse.
A border hedge of sharp piercing thorns
that formed a crown for Christ.

The painted people

From Scythia to the isle of Skye,
in the shadows of the dark ages,
Picts, the painted people
the Northern Caledonians.
At the battle of Mons Graupius
against legions of Rome
Hadrian's mighty wall could not hold them.
Carvings on serpent stones
the ring of Brodgar.
Columba's staff swept through
Dal Riada.
The Pictish twilight had begun.

Spirits lost to the breeze

Standing stones in a circle
in the late evening twilight.
spirits lost to the breeze,
a dalliance with the death knell.
Rough grey pallor of limestone,
ancient sedentary monument,
formed eons ago,
in the blind, dark depths of the sea,
from the crushed bones of the dead
that gave up their ghosts.
Henges abound on the isles
Drombeg, Bocan,
Beltany, Callanish
at the centre of the circle
the recumbent druid's altar.
Sacrificial stone,
a place of power and ritual
where the stargazer watched the night sky
in an open temple to mirror the heavens,
astral alignment
to map the celestial code,
where time and death were merged as one.

A new dawn

Crying from the valleys of shame
opening a prison of sacraments,
tearing down the walls that contain the spirit of veiled hope,
sleeping in the depths of a long-forgotten dream,
of a carousel of colours unblemished.

Spirits in the forest

A winding path,
moonlight cutting through the trees,
landing on the undergrowth.
Following the trail by the rock
of the black jaguar
towards the shabono.
Through meditation
the celestial vault is breached,
the shaman summoning the moon spirit
of the hekura,
within a dreamlike incantation
he talks like a ghost,
a superior reality is revealed.

In the cold light of day

Morning lands,
silence settles across the room,
thoughts are centred on the cold light of day
and the hours to come,
as he stares at the window,
head held low,
face in hands,
arms resting upon a dusty table,
no words are spoken,
only internal whispers.
As the clock ticks forward,
the door is opened,
he slips away.

Grianan of Aileach

The sun palace in the kingdom of Aileach,
shielding the peninsula of Inishowen,
where Eoghan was baptised by Patrick,
a majestic stronghold of the Ui Neill,
horsemen await a call to arms.
A sacred place awakened during the equinox,
stone cashel above two gleaming loughs,
tumulus and cairn solemnise the ancient ways.
A construction without corners,
where no malevolence can shroud.
Moulded by the hands of Dagda,
king of the earth and Tuatha de Dannan,
progeny of Danu,
to shelter the sepulchre of his son,
and the children of the Sidhe.

Death of a daffodil

I have lit the way for you,
now you must venture on.
Brightened your outlook
at the end of dark winter,
carried you out of the cold days.
Now you are in the cradle of the sun.
I must die and return
when the harsh winds will blow once more.

To touch the earth

We are born from the earth and we die in the earth,
to be grounded,
to touch the earth, fingers in the dark clay,
bare feet upon the damp ground,
grass between our toes,
warmth on our face from the Summer sun,
walk between the living trees in a forest,
blown by the Winter wind,
washed by the flowing river,
feel the tides turn within us,
feeling the swash and backwash of the sea,
swimming under the moon and stars,
we are born from the earth and we die in the earth,
we are one.

When all the white horses run

When all the white horses run,
when all was said but little done.
the first snows fall on Winter hill
and the evening moon shines brighter still,
piercing through the webs of time
and winds the clock, no bell to chime,
night sinks low around roof beams
And rests her head-on long-lost dreams.

Silence, smoke and solace

Smoke rising above the trees,
a new fire is lit
in the cottage by the lake,
the comforting smell of turf burning,
surrounding everything, leaving its trace
on her auburn hair, on her red coat.
She walks down the overgrown lane,
savouring the silence, finding her solace
on a path she never travelled,
but somehow feels familiar,
as if she knows the way.

The wind blows cold

The wind blows cold,
rain pouring down on old ground,
trees bend with the gust,
the last of the leaves disappear
into the dark,
the door unbolted
slams against the outhouse stone.
Inside the fire burns bright,
music streams from the radio,
the warm companionship of the voice,
no lights on in the hall,
memories on the wall.

The Queen of Bealtaine

Light the fires on Uisneach hill
to purify the driven herd
and preserve the ancient lore.
As May day dawns.
the maiden within the mortal realm
heralds the season of light.
A heady dew from the morning grass,
the lovers in the woods,
rejoice the maypole dancers.
Rowan laid upon the borders,
blessed with waters from the holy well,
hang the ribbon bough above the door.
The hawthorn bush in bloom,
flowers upon the threshold
for the floral fairy queen.

Cold comforts

No words were spoken only silence prevailed,
steps were taken as thoughts turned,
the summer air whispered through the grass,
offering a cold comfort and a momentary
respite from painful recollections.
As the evening rains began to fall,
her tears fell with them,
his awkward arm touched her shoulder,
as his head bowed down,
the heartbreak hung low.

Lost places

Once a safe shelter for loved ones,
childish laughter echoed through its halls,
songs were sung in its parlour,
secrets shared at the fire,
nurturing sleep in its bedrooms,
time passed happily within its walls.
Tears were shed at its threshold
as sons and daughters moved abroad,
letters from America on the doormat,
opened with hope and a sigh,
until there was nobody left to read them
and the house was no longer a home.

A sun dance at solstice

Midsummer, the longest day, litha
the sun at its highest point standing still,
a celebration of water, earth and sky,
the great father spirit ascends
to the reunion with his son and earth mother.
The bright half of the year has come,
dance in the Inca temple of the sun,
torch the fire by the lake shore,
to keep evil at bay,
bonfires on mountain high,
praying to the gods of the sky for rain,
to wash the ashes into the earth.
The oak king at the height of his power,
bathed in the full strength of the sun,
commands the heavens
upon the greenwood throne,
birch, fern and flowers,
St. John's Wort to chase the devil,
a triumph of light over dark,
good over evil,
magic is at its peak.
The rising of the Nile
flooding the land with fertility,
pyramids and sphinx
like the heel and slaughter stones of Stonehenge
aligned with the sun at dawn.
Nature at its most majestic,
with spirits of field, forest, river and stream,
a time of change and new beginnings,
light, warmth, strength and high energy,

before the sun star moves south
and with it the light gently grows fainter
to wane day by day.

All the light we cannot see

All the light we cannot see,
to much of it we are blinded,
stars can't shine without the darkness,
peace can't be cherished without the wildness,
to savour the long days of Summer,
we must endure the cold bleakness of Winter,
to celebrate joy we live through sorrow,
for each dark day there is a new tomorrow.

A pocketful of promises

He was hooked on a daydream
of lost opportunities.
Hanging by a thread of decency
with a pocket full of promises
and a hat full of excuses.
His feet danced a bossa nova
while his heart skipped a beat.
Waiting for the last bus home,
as the rain washed the last of his luck
down the storm drain.
The lamplight he was leaning on
caught a glint in his eye.

Blood on the rose

In the shadow of the light,
rain on stained glass windows,
grey on azure blue,
blood on the rose,
a cross on a hill,
echoes in time,
ripples in the waters.

Falling into white

Words,
drifting slowly like winged creatures
falling to earth,
filling the empty spaces,
colouring the white.

Last train to Mars

Cold coffee on the nightstand,
genuflecting in the hall,
salt Peter is up for perjury,
with no one left to call.
Mesmerising mediocrity,
has a tiger by the tail,
sanitising the monotony,
a strategy doomed to fail.
Stale water in the gutter
but stars up in the sky,
all around is intolerance,
and no one reasons why.
Sean shafted the red light,
foot down to the floor,
an angel dressed in moonlight,
came knocking on his door.
Took the bus to Alphaville,
in a land devoid of cars,
left his heart upon the windowsill
and boarded the last train to mars.

Wide eyed and restless

Following the path past the ash and the elm,
as October winds swirl fallen leaves in circles,
each step draws her deeper into the woods,
as autumn fog begins to brew
enchantment and mystery within the trees,
as the grey crow is perched upon the branch
and the banshee cry of the fox shivers the skin,
she advances wide eyed and restless
into the evening sun.

Lughnasadh

An assembly for the sun god Lugh,
son of earth and sky.
The fruits of the conjugal
have ripened and matured.
Climbing to the higher ground
closer to the heavens,
to a mountain reek.
A celebration of the battle won for the harvest
against Balor's blight.
An offering of the first fruits,
a sheaf of corn, buried in the earth at the summit,
the sacrifice of the bull and the green man
to provide new life in Spring.
Walking sunwise at the well,
east to the west to the sun.
Tying clooties to the hawthorn branch
for healing and to honour the spirit.
Halfway between the solstice and the equinox,
a festival of life and bounty,
the final of the four.
Summer is growing old,
the sun is sinking slowly in the sky
days are shortening,
the light is weakening,
moving closer to the darkness.

August rain

Light streaming on a broken picture frame,
faded colours bleed into grey,
shadows spliced upon an August branch,
night pouring down like rain outside,
An empty glass on a table
An opened letter lying still.

September

The light is weakening,
with the sun retreating.
As the year is ageing,
the scent in the air is changing.
Growth is slowing as the leaves are falling.
The days grow short and the dark hours extending.
The summer is fading
into the fall.

The white world

A moment of clear equilibrium,
the setting sun and the rising moon.
A coming of snow,
the intense frost painted the white world,
ice like a scimitar blade
spread over land and sky.
Reaching into the cold healing waters
that comes wreathing over ancient stones.

Time dances on

The border fields lie silent under the grey sky,
their earthy scent rising
like incense in a forgotten church.
The river, swollen with rain,
meanders lazily through the border clay.
Outside, the children play,
the rain-soaked earth beneath their feet.
their voices rising and falling
with the music of evening church bells,
A couple embrace in the street,
their hearts entwined
like ivy on an ancient stone wall,
their eyes alight with the fire of distant dreams.
As the day grows tired
and the sun dips below the horizon
the stars begin to shine in the night sky,
there is a sense of peace
that settles over the town like a gentle fog
and we are reminded of the beauty and the magic
that can be found in the most unexpected places.

On St. Patrick's Day,

The land awakens
with a quiet reverence,
as if the very earth itself
pays homage
to the saint who walked
these ancient hills,
the fields, once barren and cold,
now burst forth
with the vibrant green of new life.
Amidst the laughter and the songs,
there is a sense of history,
a deep-rooted connection
to the land and its people,
tales of hardship and triumph
passed down through the generations
like precious heirlooms.
Holding the past
with the promise of the future,
a palpable sense of wonder
that hangs in the air
like a melody waiting to be sung.

The hungry road

Paths of sorrow, paths of shame,
relics of a dark time,
a desolate ribbon of suffering,
shaped with the sweat of broken backs
for a shilling of Indian meal.
A futile road that leads to nowhere,
to God knows where,
dead ended,
a cruel architect,
a spectral trail etched in sadness
by gaunt, skeletal hands.
The echoes of hungry cries
that once reverberated through the hills,
the emaciated frames of workhouses,
cast long shadows over the road.
For those that fell
by the wayside of
trees bent by the breath of the wind
and those who weathered the storm.
the worn road stones
remain a silent witness
to suffering and blind indifference.

And the wind will blow us all away

Lord willing and the creek don't rise
And the wind will blow us all away
Like a red kite in the grey sky
The rains will wash over us
And the stars will be our guide
To the lights in the windows of home

The quiet thaw

In the quiet thaw between seasons,
where winter's grip reluctantly loosens,
there is a murmured promise
whispered through the boughs of slowly
awakening trees and dormant hedgerows.

It is the subtle shifting of earth and sky,
it is the arrival of spring,
tiptoeing upon the heels of winter's long farewell.

As cold yields to the tentative warmth of the sun,
the landscape emerges from its hibernation,
as if hesitantly stirring from a long slumber.

The thawing ground exhales a sigh of relief,
releasing the rivers and streams from their icy shackles.

It is a time of transition,
where the earth remembers itself anew,
it's the transformation from frost-laden mornings,
to the gentle touch of spring's awakening embrace.

In the stillness of the sleeping earth,
lies the promise of renewal,
each melting snowflake becomes a tear shed by winter,

The ground, once frozen and unyielding,
softens under the caress of sunlight,
welcoming the first tender shoots of green.

Just as winter gives way to spring,

so too do our own hearts thaw and bloom
with the promise of new beginnings.

And in this transition, we find hope,
renewal, and the enduring beauty of change.

In this delicate dance between seasons,
there is magic woven into every moment.
a reminder that even in the darkest of days,
there is always the promise of light.

Cracks in the window

The low narrow sky observed through
the cracks in the windowpane,
where cobwebs stream in the breeze
and dust dances in the shard of light
coming through the bare branches of the ash.

Flowers in the chipped blue vase,
gold speckled embellishments
around the rim,
black bolted oak table
vestiges of past lives in its rutted rind,
the hypnotic swing of the pendulum
a deep throated tessitura
in the dark.

The long winter lived
within the smoke-stained walls
of a kitchen
where now it is time to dream it up again.

The well of wisdom by the nine hazels

The salmon leap,
the final journey to the river of youth,
the spawning grounds
and rebirth.

Swimming against the current,
overcoming all adversities,
the internal locus of control,
in perfect balance,
stray not from your dreams.

From the cold northern waters
of the higher latitudes
through the depths of the Atlantic,
traveling upstream on the first flood,
rooting to the past but facing the future.

Gathering in the dark deep pools,
Connla's well of wisdom by the nine hazels,
feeding on the knowledge,
imparting it within the sacred Boyne as it swam,
fodder for Finegas, filched by Fionn.

Shoreline

A walk upon the sky road
overlooking the shore.

Waves that storm within the gale,
high tide on the high ground,
turned towards the sea.

Days are filled with the vast skies above,
pierced by streams of light
and the echo of the mountains
that carries the cries of the wind.

The mantra within

Gathered from the earth that binds us,
and fired in the heart of darkness.
shaken from the heels of seraphim angels,
prayers for the lost ones,
the hypnotic rhythm of the spoken word
to find the mantra within
the swaying drone of the song,
turn away from all your yesterdays,
and the shadows that they cast,
there are no rewards or riches
resurrected from regret.

A sacred serenade

In the heart of an autumn eve,
when raindrops dance
softly upon the windowpane,
a gentle rhythm,
a serenade from the heavens,
and in this hallowed space of warmth and light,
amidst the whispers of nature's song, they gather,
to find solace, where music intertwines with fire,
a symphony of spirits, bound by the love of the tune.

Fingers caress the strings, like whispers in the dark,
notes awaken,
rising from the depths of deep souls,
each instrument, a voice, harmonising as one,
melodies like golden threads,
weaving tales untold.

Around the hearth's embrace,
a refuge from the chill,
the fire crackles,
its warmth a tender embrace,
its amber glow illuminates eager faces,
as they surrender to the song's sweet caress,
and the world beyond the walls fades away,
lost in the ethereal realm of rhythm and melody,
in the sacred communion of hearts and minds,

And as the rain continues its nocturnal serenade,
they play on, embracing the beauty of the ephemeral,
within the sacred circle, a sanctuary where spirits soar,

as the last notes fade into the mystic night.

Before the rain set in

Living under the mountain,
days passed slow,
like forgotten dreams.

Thirty years or more
keep on, keeping on.

Looking at the last light of Summer,
Cradling in the darkness of Winter,
wishing for the green shoots of Spring.

We made our way
before the rain set in.

Changes in Modality

Love, once a steady river,
now meanders through uncharted landscapes,
joy and sorrow entwine
like vines in a garden of sentiment,
the heart discovers its capacity for resilience
and its ability to bloom anew with each passing season.
As the day turns its pages,
the changes in modality,
subtle as a breath,
profound as a heartbeat,
leave their imprints as
the world dons the cloak of reflection,
the symphony plays its final notes,
and the day dissolves into the inkwell of memory.
The architecture of belief undergoes renovations,
The air is charged with the scent of transformation,
where echoes of existence dance with the fluidity of time,
It is a dance of energies, a choreography of flux,
where the dance floor is the tapestry of existence itself,
and the windows of perception are cleansed,
the veiled moments of transition,
as the mundane transforms into the extraordinary.

From out of the cold darkness

The cold moon rises
to carry us through the darkness
and silence of the night.

A barren beauty in the landscape
the sparkle of the frost on the pathways.

A coming of snow,
the harsh cold painted the white world,
ice like a scimitar blade
spread over land and lough.

Moonlight scans the surface skin
of snow-coated fields
that reach towards the mound
upon the risen ground.

To rocky outcrops
with sleet and hail bearing down,
reaching into the cold healing waters
that comes wreathing over ancient stones
upon the batholith,
coursing down through the veins of the land,
on jagged branch and frozen hide.

Calm solitude prevails in the quietness,
from out of the cold darkness,
we shine a light under a Winter sky.
reminding us that there are better days to come.

Beyond the painted window

Beyond the painted window
the pale light stretched out
towards the February hills.

With the sky on the water,
the potent quiet of the horizon,
as you enter the outdoor,
see the trees at the water's edge
as you cross the wet ground barefoot,
sit down by the river to breathe it all,
dipping feet in the water, feeling,
exposed to the elements of faith.

A song from the rain

After the rain, the song began,
carried by a tender tide
with the rhythm of the waves
and the orchestra of the ocean
it drifted like a breeze
across hill and homestead
and danced with the sway of the branch.

Silhouetted against the full moon,
an ageless strain on the air
through keyhole and cracked windowpane
it pierced the ear drum and permeated the dream
the sweetest song ever heard,
forgotten in the dawn.

The sacred oak

The oak stands, a sacred symbol,
of wisdom, a locus of power,
a conduit for the flow of spiritual energy
between the earthly realm and the divine.

Its roots, delving deep into the earth,
anchor it firmly to the land,
grounding it in the primal energies of nature,
deep into the collective consciousness.

Yet its branches reach skyward,
touching the heavens,
bridging the realms of earth and sky.
A gateway to the otherworld,
a realm of spirits,
gods, and ancestors,
beneath its leafy canopy,
in sacred groves, rites were held,
where druids communed
with the spirits of the land.

The oak embodies the cycle of life,
death, and rebirth,
mirroring the eternal rhythms of the natural world,
in spring, its buds burst forth with new life,
In autumn, its leaves turn gold and fall,
marking the passage of time
and the inevitability of change.

The tree of Thor, God of thunder,

Cu Chulainn gained his prowess
from enchanted acorns,
Bran the Blessed possessed a magic cauldron
of sacred oak,
with power to resurrect the dead.

These days will pass

In the darkest of times,
when resistance is low,
these days will pass.

Singing to the evening sunlight,
releasing your passion to
the night's sky,
these days will pass.

A kite floating on a sea breeze,
the warm sun on your face,
these days will pass.

The crash of the waves,
the stillness of lakes,
these days will pass.

The whole of the moon,
the stars in the sky,
these days will pass.

A gathering of loved ones,
a laugh with a close friend,
these days will pass.

The Autumn colours,
the crisp cold air,
these days will pass.

A clear blue sky,
the thrill of winning,

these days will pass.

When it's all too much
and it seems there's no way out
these days will pass.

About the author

Kevin McManus is from Carrigallen, County Leitrim, Ireland. He has published a number of novels, poetry collections, a short story anthology, a play script and novellas which are all available to purchase on paperback and ebook on Amazon. In 2016 he won the Leonard award for his writing. His poems have been published in several international journals, including the London Grip, the Californian Catamaran, the Honest Ulsterman, the Fortnightly Review, the Galway Review, the Cormorant, Dreich, and An Aitiuil. In 2022 the poem "Lost Souls" was adapted into a short film and won the Blissfest film festival in Chicago. The film was also a finalist in the Cork poetry film festival and the Drumshanbo written word festival. It was also selected for the Los Angeles poetry film festival.

Other books by the author:

Poetry collection:

A cold wind from the lake

Novels:

The whole of the moon

Under the red Winter sky

Death rains down

New blood

Nine Lives

Stormforce

Dark path to Vengeance

Darkness at the edge of town

Novellas:

The night of long shadows

The haunting in the woods

Short story anthology:

The stillness of lakes

Acknowledgements

Cover image by Gordon Johnson.

Frontispiece by Jen digital art.

Yvonne Brewer for encouragement.

Attracta Fahy for advice.

Eamonn Daly for instilling in me an understanding and appreciation of poetry.

"Soundings" by Augustine Martin, still the best book to leaf through after all these years.

My wife, Mary for her patience and support, my sister Miriam and my parents, Noreen & Kevin.

Dedicated to all the daydreamers out there.

www.ingramcontent.com/pod-product-compliance
Lightning Source LLC
Chambersburg PA
CBHW021120130726

47988CB00003B/1088